for beginners

AI for Games for Beginners

Implement Artificial Intelligence Behaviors for Non-Player Characters and Game Logic

Printed in the United States of America

First Edition: 2025

This copyright page includes the necessary copyright notice, permissions request information, acknowledgments for the cover design, interior design, and editing, as well as the details of the first edition.

www.littlebiggiant.com

Introduction

Rain tapped the classroom window. A small avatar on the screen stood in a dark corridor and should have turned left. Instead it ran straight toward the player. Sam's stomach dropped. "Why won't it stop?" Sam whispered. Feet thudded in the room. Lights hummed. The avatar's path felt alive and wrong at the same time. Behind that wrongness was a real tool used in real games: A* pathfinding, first published in 1968 and still used today to guide characters through maps. That algorithm is simple to learn. It is also powerful. Games use it to move enemies, to find routes around obstacles, and to make virtual people feel like people. A famous moment in artificial intelligence history—when a computer program beat a top human player in a complex strategy game—showed how smart machines can be. Now those ideas are in games, not just in labs. The book title sits like a promise: AI for Games for Beginners — Implement Artificial Intelligence Behaviors for Non-Player Characters and Game Logic. It will show how tiny rules and clear code can change a game world. It will show how a calm line of instructions can turn a stuck enemy into a clever opponent.

Sam leaned closer. Sweat cooled on the neck. The avatar paused, then pivoted exactly where a hidden rule told it to. Sam realized the problem was not the map or the sprite. It was the behavior logic. Fear and curiosity mixed into a single question that would not go away: if one small rule could make an enemy chase, what could a few more rules make the whole world do?

Table of Contents

Chapter 1

Foundations of Game AI

Step 1: What game AI is and how it differs from academic AI

In games, AI is about making computer-controlled characters feel alive and useful within a playable world. It is not about solving every hard problem in artificial intelligence or proving mathematical theorems. Instead, game AI focuses on practical, fast, and reliable behavior that supports fun, challenge, and immersion. Think of it as a toolkit for believable actions in real-time, where decisions must be timely, easy to understand, and easy to adjust based on how a game feels when you play it.

This kind of AI often uses simple, repeatable patterns rather than exhaustive search for the perfect answer. For example, many NPCs use patterns like patrol, investigate, and respond to threats. The goal is not to find the absolute best move in every situation, but to provide moves that feel appropriate, consistent, and learnable by the player. Real-time constraints matter a lot in games. NPCs must decide quickly enough to keep the game flowing. They might not always choose the "optimal" action in a theoretical sense, but they usually choose actions that fit the moment, the story, and the player's expected experience.

You'll also see common techniques that are widely used in game AI, such as finite state machines, behavior trees, and pathfinding. Finite state machines, or FSMs, let an agent switch between a small number of clear states—like patrolling, chasing, or waiting—and define rules for when to move between those states. Behavior trees organize decisions in a tree-like structure that can be easier to read and modify as a game grows. Pathfinding finds a way for a character to move from point A to point B while avoiding obstacles. These tools work together to create scenes that feel purposeful rather than random.

Micro-case: A castle guard on patrol

Imagine a guard walking a short route with occasional stops to look around. The guard has a simple FSM with states: patrol, investigate, and return. If a loud noise is heard, the guard transitions from patrol to investigate. If the guard spots the player in light, the rule-set might shift the guard into chase or call for backup. If nothing happens after a time, the guard returns to patrol. This isn't the search for a perfect path in a maze; it's a reliable pattern that players learn to read. The result is a scene that feels responsive and fair, not chaotic or random. You can tweak how long the guard investigates, how strongly sight lines are treated, or how quickly backup arrives, all without rewriting the whole system.

This approach is deliberate. It prioritizes clarity, speed, and testability over theoretical completeness. By using repeatable rules and well-defined states, you can audit behavior, find bugs quickly, and adjust the feel of the game with small changes. When you design game AI, you're designing experiences: how the world responds to players, how NPCs convey personality, and how the rules of the game shape choices.

Step 2: Roles of NPCs, enemies, allies, and systemic game logic

Non-player characters fall into several roles in most games, and each role helps build the world in a different way. NPCs (like townsfolk, shopkeepers, or quest givers) provide flavor, information, and services. Enemies offer challenge and risk, pushing the player to adapt and grow. Allies, or companions, can assist the player by sharing abilities, information, or buffs. Systemic game logic is the hidden framework that coordinates how all these pieces fit together across scenes, quests, economy, and progression. It's the rules engine that keeps the world coherent as players make choices.

NPCs can be predictable in a way that serves the game's pace. A farmer who tends crops, a guard who patrols a district, or a healer who appears when you need aid should behave in ways players can reasonably expect. Enemies should present a fair challenge, not an impossible puzzle. Allies should be reliable enough to feel supportive but not so powerful that the game loses challenge. Systemic logic binds these roles to larger goals: guiding the player's journey, enforcing quest conditions, and shaping the world's reactions to the player's actions.

A simple rule helps: roles are more than individual behaviors. They are the pieces that interact through shared rules and events. When a player completes a quest, the shopkeeper might unlock a new item; when a day ends, a new enemy spawns or a merchant changes stock; when an ally takes action, it can unlock a new path or reveal information. These interactions create a living world where every character supports the overall experience.

Micro-case: A quest-giving merchant

Picture a merchant who offers a quest only after the player has helped a certain number of villagers. The merchant's behavior isn't random; it depends on a small set of conditions: player progress, stock level, and perhaps the time of day. The quest offered is not arbitrary; it follows a story thread that fits the world's rhythm. This is an example of systemic logic at work: a single NPC delivering content in a way that feels natural, connected to prior events, and meaningful to the player's journey. You can adjust when the quest appears, what the reward is, and how often the merchant cycles through options to maintain balance and interest.

Another micro-case: +Coordination among enemies

In a small group of enemies, you might see a tiny choreography: a lead foe draws attention, another moves to flank, and a third calls for reinforcements when the player fights back. The on-screen motion is not a random sequence; it's a designed pattern that creates tension and texture. The pattern should be readable enough for players to learn, yet varied enough to stay engaging. Systemic logic stores these coordination rules so the same behavior plays out consistently across different maps and scenes.

Step 3: Design constraints: performance, predictability, and player experience

Performance matters because games run in real time. AI that eats too much CPU or memory can cause stuttering, higher frame times, or longer load screens. The design choice is to keep AI lightweight for most characters, using simple decision trees, ready-made patterns, and infrequent full evaluations. For more important NPCs or for scenes where the player's experience depends on the AI's quality, you can increase the fidelity a little, but you still keep it within a budget that preserves smooth gameplay. A practical approach is to tier AI complexity: far-off or nonessential NPCs use lean logic that updates less often, while key characters use richer behavior that updates more frequently.

Predictability is the sense that players can learn and anticipate how NPCs will act. Predictable behavior helps players plan, master the game, and feel clever for solving challenges. You don't want to remove all surprise, but you do want to avoid confusing patterns or abrupt, unexplained moves. For example, a guard that suddenly turns invisible or a merchant that acts out of character can break immersion because players cannot reason about that behavior within the game's rules. Instead, give clear cues: if the guard is coming closer, you should notice the guard's posture or a warning tone. If the merchant becomes unavailable after a quest is completed, the change should be visible in the world, not a hidden secret.

Player experience is the heart of design constraints. The AI should support the player's goals, not obstruct them. It should feel fair, challenging, and legible. You balance difficulty by shaping patterns, timing, and response ranges. You tune how quickly enemies react, how often allies offer help, and how environmental cues reveal the world's rules. A well-tuned AI system rewards learning: players feel smarter when they recognize a pattern and act on it, rather than feeling lucky or cheated by random luck.

To ground these ideas, consider three practical practices:

- Use clear, simple rule sets for most characters. Simple rules are easier to test, tweak, and explain to players.

- Schedule heavy AI tasks for moments that matter most. Let quiet scenes run lighter logic; reserve more complex decisions for critical encounters or key story beats.

- Build feedback into design. Observe how players react to NPC behavior in playtests, and adjust patterns to improve clarity and enjoyment.

Two additional micro-cases illustrate the design constraints in action

Micro-case A: A patroller with a predictable cycle

A guard follows a three-state cycle: patrol, stop to scan, and return. The cycle is visible enough for players to learn, so they can anticipate the guard's location and timing. If the player is spotted, the guard shifts to chase. If the player hides behind a pillar, the guard resumes patrol after a short search, then returns to the original route. The result is a dependable, learnable pattern that keeps the scene fair and engaging. If the player's skill increases, the guard's response can be slightly tightened, or a backup unit can be introduced to restore challenge without breaking the sense of structure.

Micro-case B: The quest-averse ally

An ally who accompanies the player on an exploration quest uses a simple heuristic: follow, slightly lag behind, and use a protective shield when the player heads into danger. If the player ignores the ally or moves too fast, the ally might fall back to a safe position, but never disappear. The ally's behavior is easy to predict, which helps players coordinate actions in combat or exploration. If the player completes the quest, the ally's support patterns shift—sometimes offering new dialogue or a reward path—without surprising the player with an unexplained change.

Key Takeaway: Game AI uses simple, reliable patterns and clear design constraints to create believable, enjoyable experiences. By focusing on real-time practicality, legible behavior, and well-balanced interactions among NPCs, enemies, allies, and systemic logic, you build worlds that feel alive and fair.

Coming up next: Architectures and Data Models

Chapter 2

Architectures and Data Models

Core data structures and algorithms used by game AI

You start with simple building blocks. The most common data structures in game AI are graphs, grids, and lists. A graph is a map of points (nodes) and connections (edges) that show how you can move from one place to another. In a game, graphs often represent walkable areas, waypoints, or navmeshes. A grid is a regular array, like a chessboard or a city map broken into squares. Grids are easy to reason about and fast to scan, which makes them handy for small-to-medium maps. Lists and arrays store things you know about, like a group of enemies or a queue of tasks.

Two widely used ideas live inside these structures: search algorithms and ordering systems. Search algorithms help determine paths or plans. A line of play might use Dijkstra's or A *search to find the best route from where you are to where you want to be. Dijkstra's algorithm finds the shortest path from one point to all others in a graph, while A* adds a small hint (a heuristic) about which direction looks most promising, so you reach your destination faster. In practice, A* is the go-to choice for real-time games because it balances speed with sensible paths.

To decide what to do next in a moment of action, you often need a quick way to pick from several options. That's where priority queues come in. A priority queue stores tasks or goals and always serves the highest-priority item first. If a guard sees danger, a high-priority decision—like pursuing the player or calling for backup—jumps ahead of routine patrol steps.

Another familiar friend is BFS, a simple search that uses a queue to explore a map in layers. It's not the fastest for every task, but it's predictable and easy to reason about. DFS, which uses a stack, is good for exhaustive exploration in smaller puzzles or for games that want a "search deeply" flavor.

If you're working with a moving character on a large map, you'll also touch on spatial data structures that help find neighbors quickly. A handful of common approaches include grids, octrees, and simple spatial hashing. These structures help your AI answers questions like, "Who is near me?" or "What area should I check next?" without scanning every tile or every enemy.

Now, two concrete, kid-friendly examples to see these ideas in action.

Example 1: The rogue NPC and pathfinding. An NPC needs to reach a player while dodging walls and traps. The game builds a graph of walkable spots and uses A *to find the path. The path is then followed step by step, with the NPC's movement system turning the plan into motion. If the player runs behind a pillar, the system can re-run A* from the current position to adjust the route. This shows how a tiny decision—the choice of a path—depends on a bigger network of options and a fast rule to pick the best one.

Example 2: A patrol routine on a grid. A guard walks a fixed route that visits several waypoints. The game stores these waypoints in a simple list and uses BFS to plan every leg of the patrol if a disruption happens (like a door opening somewhere else). If a loud noise occurs, the guard can switch to a short, direct path toward the source, then resume the loop. The data structures here keep the logic clean: one list of waypoints, one small search to re-route when needed.

These core structures and algorithms aren't flashy, but they're steady. They give you predictable behavior, which helps players feel the world is real and responsive. The trick is to match the tool to the task: a large, open map might benefit from a navmesh and A* with a good heuristic; a tiny puzzle game can use a simple grid with BFS for quick, understandable navigation.

A few practical notes to keep things smooth:

- Keep your open and closed lists small and local. Don't keep a big global map in memory if your map is huge; recalculate when needed instead of smoking the processor with constant updates.

- Choose your heuristic carefully. A good heuristic guides you toward the goal without promising things you can't deliver. If you're unsure, start with a simple straight-line estimate and test how it feels in play.

- Cache repeated calculations when possible. If a path is reused often, store it briefly and reuse it unless something in the world changes.

- Balance realism with performance. Real-time games can look smoother if you simplify distant decisions or approximate paths rather than calculating perfect routes every frame.

Entity-component and agent architectures for modular behavior

Think of an entity as a label, like "NPC-01." An entity itself carries no behavior; it is just an ID. The behavior comes from components—small, focused data containers that describe what the entity can be or do. For example, a simple guard might have components like Position, Velocity, Health, Sight, and PatrolRoute. The same set of components can describe a friendly ally or a sneaky scout by adding or removing a couple of pieces. Systems read the components and act on them, creating the behavior you see in the game.

This separation is the core idea behind an entity-component system (ECS). It helps you mix and match abilities without rewriting big chunks of code. It also makes testing easier: you can swap out or mock specific components without disturbing the whole NPC.

You could say an agent is a small decision-maker built from modular parts. An agent uses its components and perhaps a few behavior modules to decide what to do next. For example, a basic AI agent might use:

- Position and Velocity to move

- Sight to detect players or objects

- Intent or Goal components to track what it wants to accomplish

- A Behavior component that says whether to patrol, chase, or hide

Two practical examples help show how this works in practice.

Example 1: A patrol-guard with modular behavior. The NPC has Position, Velocity, Health, and PatrolRoute components, plus a Behavior module that knows how to switch between "Patrolling" and "Chasing." A MovementSystem reads Position and Velocity to update the guard's location. A SightSystem uses the Sight component to detect a player; when detection happens, the Behavior module changes the state from "Patrolling" to "Chasing." The same systems work on different guards because the behavior logic is packaged as modular components. Remove or swap a module, and the guard changes role without reworking the whole AI.

Example 2: A friendly helper with flexible tactics. A companion NPC has components for Position, Health, Inventory, and a simple AI module that can switch between "Follow Player" and "Assist." If the player picks up an item, the Inventory component updates, and the AI can decide whether to carry items, drop them, or give them to the player. This modular arrangement makes it easy to expand the companion's skills later—just add a new component and a small behavior rule, not a whole rewrite.

Why this approach helps you, especially in games for younger players or learners:

- Modularity makes it easier to experiment. You can add new ideas—like a different chase pattern or a new kind of ally—without tearing apart existing code.

- Reuse saves time. The same MovementSystem can work for enemy and ally NPCs with different components.

- Testing becomes simpler. You can test one component in isolation and then see how it interacts with others.

A few practical tips for ECS-minded design:

- Keep components small and singular in purpose. A component should describe one fact, not many. If it grows too big, split it.

- Separate what happens from how it happens. Systems drive the behavior; components hold the data the systems need.

- Document how components relate. A simple map showing which systems read or write which components helps you avoid silent bugs.

- Guard performance with batching. If many NPCs share the same movement or decision logic, run those updates together to save cycles.

Communication patterns: events, blackboards, and messaging systems

Having many NPCs and systems all talking at once can get noisy. Clear patterns help keep conversations predictable and debuggable.

Events

Events are like loud shouts that many listeners can hear. An event describes something that happened, and any system that cares about that event can respond. For example, an event called PlayerDetected might trigger alarms, switch a gunner's behavior, or spawn reinforforcements. The advantage is immediacy and decoupling: the sender doesn't need to know who will react. The downside is the risk of too many listeners reacting to too many events, which can create chaos if not managed carefully.

Blackboards

A blackboard is a shared memory space where systems can read and write data. Think of it as a whiteboard that all AI teammates can look at and update. The blackboard might hold values like "enemyNearby," "lastKnownPosition," or "dangerLevel." When a system sees a change, it can update the board, and other systems can respond to that new state. The benefit is a centralized source of truth that prevents every system from duplicating work. The risk is contention and stale data if different parts of the game update the board at cross-purposes or out of sync.

Messaging systems

Direct messages or a message queue let NPCs talk to one another in a controlled way. A message might say, “Guard A, pursue target,” or “Scout, report status.” Messaging is precise and easy to trace in debugging because you can follow the path of a particular message. The challenge is avoiding tight coupling: if messages become too specific, you end up weaving a web of tiny dependencies that’s hard to change later.

Two short, concrete scenarios to ground these patterns:

Scenario A: A storm of events. A loud crash on the other side of a hall fires an event named DoorCrash. The Event system immediately notifies nearby guards and a body of alarms. Some agents switch to a defensive stance; others rush to investigate; a few do both in sequence. The advantage is rapid, visible reaction that feels alive. The risk is too many events piling up, causing performance issues or confusing player experience if events aren't well filtered.

Scenario B: A shared world state. A blackboard holds "PlayerVisible" and "NoiseLevel." A stealth NPC checks NoiseLevel to decide whether to move quietly or sprint, while a guard uses PlayerVisible to decide when to call for backup. If a new piece of data updates, the board notifies subsystems that care, but the data stays singular and current. This approach is tidy and predictable, helping you tune difficulty and pacing.

A few practical tips to keep patterns healthy:

- Establish a clear event taxonomy. Have a predictable naming scheme and a reasonable maximum number of listeners per event.

- Refresh the blackboard thoughtfully. Don't flood it with every little piece of data; prioritize what truly changes behavior.

- Use direct messages for essential, specific requests. Reserve broad broadcasts for broad, player-facing outcomes.

- Build in the ability to log or replay messages. Seeing what happened and when helps you diagnose why an NPC acted a certain way.

Key Takeaway: Modular data structures and clean communication patterns let you mix and match behaviors, scale NPC variety, and keep debugging manageable.

Coming up next Subtittle: Finite State Machines and Behavior Trees

1) Building reactive behaviors with finite state machines,

2) Composing complex actions using behavior trees,

3) Designing transitions, debugging flows, and testability at the very end.

Chapter 3

Finite State Machines and Behavior Trees

You design a small, responsive brain for your characters by using finite state machines (FSMs). An FSM is a simple map of states and the rules that move your NPCs from one state to another. Each state represents a behavior the NPC can perform, and transitions are the moments when the NPC switches behaviors. The idea is straightforward:

stay in a given mode until something changes, then switch to a new mode that fits the new situation.

Step 1: Define the states you need

Begin with a short list of the core behaviors your NPC will display. For a guard, you might choose: Patrolling, Alert, Chasing, and Attacking. For a cleaner example, think of a merchant: Idle, Browse, Trade, and Evade. Each state should describe a clear, observable behavior. Don't crowd your machine with dozens of tiny states; aim for meaningful, durable modes that cover most situations you expect the NPC to encounter.

Rationale: Simple, well-chosen states keep the FSM readable and predictable. If you find yourself creating more states than you can manage, you probably need to merge some or redefine your transitions so the machine remains comprehensible.

Step 2: List the transitions and triggers

For every pair of states that can connect, write down what triggers the transition. Common triggers are the player entering line of sight, a loud noise, low health, reaching a waypoint, or losing the target. Don't omit edge cases—like what happens if the target disappears while chasing. Record prioritization rules: if multiple triggers fire at once, which transition wins? A crisp priority order prevents jittery or contradictory behavior.

Rationale: Clear triggers and priorities prevent your NPCs from flitting between states in unpredictable ways. They also make debugging easier because you can point to a specific trigger when something goes wrong.

Step 3: Implement transitions with guard conditions

Turn your map into code or a visual diagram. Each transition should have a guard condition—an explicit rule that must be true for the transition to occur. Keep guards small and check them in the order of priority you defined. If a guard isn't met, the NPC stays in its current state. That restraint avoids "flip-flop" behavior where the NPC keeps bouncing between two states.

Rationale: Guard conditions discipline transitions. They keep movement from becoming erratic, which is essential for player trust and for believable AI.

Step 4: Test with simple scenarios

Create a handful of test situations and run them through your FSM. For example, a scenario where a guard patrols, hears a noise, sees the player, and then loses sight. Each step should follow the exact transitions you laid out. If the test breaks, trace the path of states and check each guard condition. Make small, incremental fixes so you can see which change made the difference.

Rationale: Testing with controlled scenarios helps you verify your logic before you layer on more complexity. It also makes it easier to spot transitions that are missing or misordered.

Micro-case 1: A guard on patrol

The guard starts in Patrol. The first trigger is "see player," which moves the guard to Chasing. While chasing, if the guard closes within attack range, the trigger shifts to Attacking. If the player escapes sight, the guard moves to Alert for a moment, then back to Patrol if the player remains unseen. The pattern is straightforward, but the rules are the backbone: see player → Chasing; close in → Attacking; lose sight → Alert → Patrol.

Micro-case 2: A tired healer in a game town

In Idle, the healer moves to Browse when not needed, then to Trade if a customer approaches. If a monster appears (sudden danger), the guard transitions to Evade or Call for Help as needed. This simple example shows how a few well-chosen states and guards create lifelike behavior without overcomplicating the logic.

What can go wrong with FSMs—and how to fix it

- They get stuck in a state: Add a safe default transition or a "fallback" guard that moves the NPC to a neutral state if nothing else triggers.

- Transitions are missed: Revisit your triggers to ensure every possible situation has a path, even if it's a minimal one like "return to Patrol."

- Jittery behavior: Introduce a small delay or minimum time in a state before a transition can occur, or add hysteresis to guard checks.

Tools and templates you can copy

- FSM design template

States: [Idle, Patrol, Alert, Chase, Attack]

Transitions:

- Idle → Patrol when time elapses

- Patrol → Alert when a suspicious sound is heard

- Alert → Patrol if nothing is seen after a short wait

- Alert → Chase when the target is spotted

- Chase → Attack when in range

- Chase → Patrol if the target escapes sight

Guard conditions: SeeTarget, HeardSound, InRange, LostTarget

- Quick-checklist for FSMs

1) Are all states necessary and meaningful?

2) Does every transition have a guard?

3) Is there a default path if no triggers fire?

4) Have I tested at least three contrasting scenarios?

Two short examples show the steps in action

Example A: Guard with patrol and chase

- Step 1: Choose states Patrol, Alert, Chase, Attack.

- Step 2: Add triggers: SeeTarget, LoseTarget, InRange, LoseSight.

- Step 3: Define order of guards to prevent conflicts: SeeTarget first, then InRange, then LoseTarget.

- Step 4: Test scenarios: normal patrol, wind-up alert when hearing a strange sound, chase when target is seen, attack when in range.

Example B: Merchant with simple reactions

- Step 1: States Idle, Browse, Trade, Evade.

- Step 2: Triggers: PlayerApproaches, TradeRequest, ThreatDetected.

- Step 3: Ensure priority so threat triggers Evade even if the merchant was in Trade.

- Step 4: Run a few tests: calm day, customer arrives, merchant trades, thief appears, merchant evades.

Key takeaway (the single lesson you can carry forward)

Key Takeaway: A clear, small set of states and precise guards make NPCs predictable, adaptable, and easy to debug without losing the feeling of a living world.

Designing transitions, debugging flows, and testability

Transitions tell your NPCs when to switch gears, so you must design them with clarity and caution. A robust transition system makes behavior feel intentional rather than random. When transitions are messy, your AI can act in ways that feel uncanny or inconsistent, which breaks immersion.

Step 1: Map transitions with care

Draw a simple map of states and the exact triggers that move between them. Include guard conditions for every arrow and note any priority rules. A map is a blueprint you can return to whenever you expand the AI. It also helps you communicate your design to teammates.

Rationale: A plan you can physically see reduces miscommunication and helps you spot gaps before you code.

Step 2: Build lightweight tests for transitions

Create quick, repeatable tests that validate one transition at a time. For example, test that “SeeTarget” reliably yields Chase, and that “LostTarget” returns to Patrol. Use a timer or step counter to ensure transitions don’t fire too soon or too late. When possible, automate these tests so you can run them after changes.

Rationale: Tests are your early warning system. They catch regressions and keep your AI honest as you add features.

Step 3: Add visibility and simple debugging tools

Keep a simple log that records each state entry, exit, and the trigger that caused a switch. If your engine supports visualization, show a small, real-time diagram of the current state and upcoming transitions. This makes it much easier to identify where the path is going wrong during playtests.

Rationale: Seeing the brain in action reduces guesswork and speeds iteration.

Step 4: Refine with playful experimentation

Try small changes and compare outcomes. Increase sensitivity to a trigger in one test and later reduce it if it creates jitter. The goal isn't to be perfect at once but to move toward a balance between responsiveness and stability.

Two micro-cases demonstrate design and debugging

Micro-case 3: Ambiguous audio

- Step 1: Add a new trigger: HeardThreatSound.

- Step 2: Create a new path: Patrol → Alert when sound is heard, even if the target isn't seen.

- Step 3: Test: play the sound twice in quick succession; ensure the NPC doesn’t flip between Alert and Patrol too often.

Micro-case 4: Attack chain misfire

- Step 1: The AI sometimes re-enters Chase while Attacking due to a fast sighting reset.

- Step 2: Introduce a short “in-attack” lockout to prevent re-entry into Chase while attacking.

- Step 3: Run through a sequence where the target briefly disappears and reappears; verify the AI remains steady in Attack or returns to Chase only after a clear trigger.

Putting it all together: a practical approach to debugging and testing

- Start small: build a simple FSM with 3–4 states and 2–3 transitions.

- Expand gradually: add one state or one transition at a time and test after each change.

- Stay disciplined: document guards, states, and priorities so future you understands the design.

- Favor readability over cleverness: a slightly longer but crystal-clear FSM is easier to maintain and debug than a compact but tangled one.

Tools and templates you can copy

- Behavior touchpoints template

1) State names: Idle, Patrol, Alert, Chase, Attack

2) Triggers: SeeTarget, LostTarget, InRange, HeardSound

3) Guard conditions: targetVisible, targetInRange, pathClear

4) Priority order: SeeTarget > InRange > LostTarget

5) Default path: If nothing else fires, return to Patrol

- Behavior Tree skeleton

Root

- Selector

- Sequence: SeeTarget -> Chase -> Attack

- Sequence: Wander -> LookAround

- Fallback: PatrolRoute

- Action nodes: MoveToWaypoint, LookAround, AttackTarget, Evade

- Quick diagnostic checklist

1) Do you have a clear definition for every state?

2) Are all transitions guarded?

3) Is there a default path if nothing triggers?

4) Have you tested at least three different gameplay scenarios?

Exercises

1) FSM sketch and test (15–20 minutes): Draw a 4-state FSM on paper for an NPC of your choice. List all transitions and guards. Explain in 2–3 sentences what each transition accomplishes.

2) Behavior Tree bootstrap (20–30 minutes): Create a tiny BT with a top-level Sequence that includes MoveTo, Wait, and ReactToPlayer. Run through three possible player actions and note how the tree responds.

3) Transition debugging race (10–15 minutes): Simulate two conflicting triggers at once (e.g., SeeTarget and HeardSound). Decide which should win and adjust guards accordingly. Verify the result by stepping through the scenario in your mind or with a simple script.

4) Quick verifier (5–10 minutes): Review an existing AI you've built. List every state and each transition's guard. Ensure there is at least one path for every possible situation you can define in your game world.

Troubleshooting quick fixes

- The AI stays in one state too long: add a minimum time in the current state and require a real trigger to move out.

- The AI flickers between states (jitter): introduce a small delay or hysteresis on guard checks to prevent rapid flips.

- A transition fires but the behavior doesn't feel right: check the order of guard evaluation and ensure you don't have conflicting guards that can both be true at the same moment.

- The AI ignores a player when in sight: verify your targetVisible condition is updated promptly and that there is no early return to a safe state before the chase begins.

Coming up next

Pathfinding and World Representation

1) Grid, waypoint, and navmesh representations for navigation,

2) Implementing A* and optimizing search for large maps,

3) Hierarchical pathfinding and runtime path refinement

Coming up next: Pathfinding and World Representation

Grid, waypoint, and navmesh representations for navigation,

Implementing A* and optimizing search for large maps,

Hierarchical pathfinding and runtime path refinement

Chapter 4

Pathfinding and World Representation

By the end of this chapter you will understand three navigation representations (grid, waypoint graphs, and navmeshes), how to run A* on those maps, and how to use hierarchical pathfinding to keep pathfinding fast on larger worlds.

1) Grid, waypoint, and navmesh representations for navigation

There are three common ways to tell a game's characters where they can move. Each has strengths and trade-offs, and the best choice often depends on the game type and map design.

Grid representations turn the world into a checkerboard of cells. Each cell knows whether it is walkable and, sometimes, a small cost to move through. Grids are great for tile-based games and for maps that are naturally aligned to a uniform grid. They're simple to store in memory as a 2D array and easy to reason about with math like coordinates and row/column indices.

Waypoint graphs place nodes at important spots—doors, corners, intersections, or places where NPCs tend to turn. Edges connect nearby nodes and have costs that reflect distance or difficulty. Waypoints are efficient for large, open spaces or interiors where you don't want a dense grid. They let you keep only the essential routes, which can save memory and speed up searches in big maps.

Navmeshes slice walkable space into convex polygons. Movement stays on the surface of these polygons, and you travel across shared edges between neighboring polygons. Navmeshes give you natural movement that follows the actual layout of the level (walls, corridors, open rooms) and work well for complex geometry. They can be more involved to generate, but they map well to believable character motion.

When deciding which to use, ask: Do I need pixel-perfect ground truth (grid)? Do I want a compact graph that preserves key routes (waypoints)? Or do I want smooth, geometry-aware movement over a complex space (navmesh)? Each choice changes how you build data structures, run algorithms, and optimize performance.

In practice, many games blend approaches. A city map might use a navmesh for smooth ground movement in streets and plazas, a grid overlay for indoor rooms with tight navigation, and a handful of waypoint anchors for important chokepoints. The important thing is to know how your representation changes the steps you take to find a path.

Two short examples help illustrate. Example A: A 10-by-10 tile dungeon with walls creates a dense grid. If you mark each tile as walkable or blocked, you can run pathfinding by moving from one walkable tile to any neighboring walkable tile. It's straightforward and predictable. Example B: A large outdoor level with several buildings uses a small set of waypoints at doorways and plaza nodes. NPCs can hop from one node to another along pre-defined edges, which reduces search space and keeps NPC motion feeling purposeful rather than jittery in wide-open areas. In both cases, the representation you choose shapes the steps you take next.

2) Grid representations for navigation

A grid map is built from a matrix of cells. Each cell has coordinates (x, y) and a flag for walkability. For performance, you store a simple walkable flag, sometimes a movement cost (for rough terrain), and perhaps a few dynamic obstacles that can flip a cell from walkable to blocked during gameplay.

To use a grid with pathfinding, you usually connect each cell to its up to four or eight neighbors. The most common approach is four neighbors (north, south, east, west); eight neighbors adds diagonals, which makes paths shorter but can complicate movement costs and collision checks. The cost to move between adjacent cells is typically the same, or slightly higher for diagonal moves to reflect longer distance.

Key considerations include cell size and map updates. A smaller cell size yields higher precision but more cells to track; a larger cell size reduces memory and search time but can miss narrow passages. Dynamic obstacles—like a door that closes—must be updated in the grid quickly so NPCs do not attempt to move through blocked cells.

A practical micro-example: imagine a small 6-by-6 grid with a single wall row splitting the space. You can still move from any start to any goal by stepping around the wall. If you scale up to a 60-by-60 grid, the search space grows, so you'll want to optimize how you store the grid and how you search it, or switch to a more compact representation like a graph of waypoints for longer runs.

3) Waypoint representations for navigation

A waypoint graph is built by placing nodes at meaningful places: doorways, intersections, or regions that NPCs routinely navigate between. Each node connects to nearby nodes with edges that have costs, usually representing distance or traversal difficulty. The map's topology—long corridors, open rooms, and narrow passages—drives your node placement.

To use a waypoint graph for pathfinding, you run the search on the graph rather than the entire grid. The graph is smaller, so searches are faster, which is especially helpful in large environments. A typical approach is to connect nodes with two kinds of costs: a straight-line distance if the path between two nodes is unobstructed, and an actual traversal cost if movement requires turning or going through a door or narrow corridor. If the graph is not fully connected, you add edges only where a valid movement path exists.

One practical micro-example: a museum map with several rooms connected by doors. Place nodes at each doorway and at key hallway junctions. An NPC deciding from a lobby to the exit would hop from node to node along the shortest route via doorways, rather than checking every possible tile in a large hall.

4) Navmesh representations for navigation

A navmesh partitions walkable space into a set of convex polygons, typically triangles or quads. The polygons fit the level geometry, so paths follow natural routes around walls and obstacles. A path through a navmesh usually goes from polygon to neighboring polygon via shared edges. This produces smooth movement and helps avoid awkward, zig-zagging paths that sometimes occur with grids.

Navmeshes work best when you need movement that respects the exact shape of the level. They can be heavier to generate, and you may need a small graph to connect polygons for quick lookups. However, for realistic movement across complex rooms and corridors, navmeshes often outperform grids in both realism and performance, especially when you scale to large environments.

A practical micro-example: in a cathedral-like interior, the navmesh creates long, flowing routes along broad aisles rather than jumping across a maze of small steps. An AI agent follows a path by stepping from polygon to polygon, which feels natural and visually believable.

5) Implementing A* and optimizing search for large maps

A* is the go-to pathfinding algorithm for many game AI systems because it balances optimality and speed. It maintains two sets: an open set of nodes to explore and a closed set of nodes already evaluated. Each node tracks a cost from the start (g), and a total estimated cost to the goal (f = g + h), where h is a heuristic estimate of the remaining distance.

Start by choosing a representation for the graph you're searching (grid cells, waypoint graph, or navmesh polygons). Then assign costs for moving from one node to another. Use a simple heuristic that makes sense for the map: Manhattan distance for grid-based, Euclidean distance when you want a straight-line feel, or a domain-specific heuristic that respects movement constraints.

A small example: in a 7-by-7 grid with a few walls, start at the bottom-left and aim for the top-right. The algorithm adds the start cell to the open set, then repeatedly pulls the lowest f-score node, expands its neighbors, updates costs, and moves nodes to the closed set until it reaches the goal. You'll reconstruct the path by tracing back from the goal to the start through parent pointers.

To optimize for larger maps, you can use a few practical tricks. Use a fast priority queue (binary heap or similar) for the open set. Cache repeated results for common start-goal pairs if that makes sense for your game. If the map has regions with little or no change, you can reuse previous search results or partially reuse the path when NPCs slide between similar routes. Be aware of pathological maps where many nodes have similar f-scores; add a small tie-breaker favoring closer nodes to the goal to reduce jitter in movement.

6) Hierarchical pathfinding and runtime path refinement

When maps become large, a single A* search can still be heavy. Hierarchical pathfinding tackles this by dividing the map into regions and solving a two-layer problem: a coarse path across regions, then a finer path inside each region.

First, you create a higher-level graph where each region is a node and inter-region connections are edges. To move from A to B, you find a coarse route across this regional graph. Then you refine the route inside each region to a detailed subpath that connects the entry and exit points through the region's internal graph (grid, waypoint graph, or navmesh polygons). This reduces search space dramatically and keeps NPCs moving smoothly across large maps.

Runtime path refinement lets NPCs adapt when obstacles appear after a path is chosen. If a door closes or a crowd blocks a corridor, the NPC can re-plan locally, within the current region or in a nearby region, rather than re-running a full map-wide search. This keeps behavior responsive while preserving performance.

Two micro-examples to illustrate: (1) A city block divided into neighborhoods. The NPC's path goes from neighborhood A to B via a few regional links, then a precise local route within the destination neighborhood. (2) A castle with multiple courtyards. The NPC chooses a high-level route across courtyards, then computes exact steps on the route's path inside each courtyard, adjusting if a gate becomes blocked.

7) Examples and micro-cases that show the steps in action

- Case 1: A dungeon map uses a grid representation. You mark walls as blocked, assign uniform movement costs to open cells, and run A* to find a path between two rooms. The result is a crisp sequence of moves through open cells that respects walls.

- Case 2: An outdoor level uses a waypoint graph. Nodes sit at crossroads and entrances; edges reflect the easiest crossings. A* runs on the graph, returning a route that uses doors and open spaces, often shorter in memory usage than a dense grid path. The NPC travels from start to goal by hopping between waypoints, then uses a short local search to fine-tune the exact ground path.

Troubleshooting: common problems and quick fixes

- Problem: The path often looks wrong or clips through walls. Quick fix: verify your walkability data for the map and ensure neighboring relationships reflect actual movement constraints for your chosen representation.

- Problem: The search runs slowly on large maps. Quick fix: switch to a hierarchical approach, reduce the grid cell size, or switch to a waypoint/navmesh representation for the large-scale search and use local refinements.

- Problem: NPCs take wildly different routes to the same destination in repeated plays. Quick fix: apply a small tie-breaker in your heuristic to prefer closer nodes or introduce a deterministic ordering for equally scored nodes.

- Problem: Dynamic obstacles force frequent re-planning. Quick fix: implement local re-planning within the current region or neighborhood and reuse previous path segments when feasible.

Tools, templates, and quick-start templates

- Grid pathfinding template: a small grid map with a walkable flag per cell, a neighbor function for four directions, and a basic A* implementation with a binary-heap queue.

- Waypoint graph template: a node list with coordinates, an adjacency list, and a simple A* over the graph with edge costs.

- Navmesh template: a polygon list with neighbors, a helper to pick a start polygon and a goal polygon, and a lightweight A* variant over polygons.

Exercises

1) In 15 minutes, sketch a 6-by-6 grid with three walls. Mark walkable cells and practice tracing a path from bottom-left to top-right by hand. Measure how many steps your path uses and note any detours caused by walls.

2) Draw a small waypoint graph with five nodes and four edges. Create a simple start and end pair and run a mental A* pass. Compare the path you imagined with the straight-line distance between start and end.

3) Take a tiny map (grid or graph) and implement a basic A* on paper or in a lightweight notebook script. Record the number of nodes expanded and the path length. Try a different heuristic and compare results.

4) Divide a simple map into two regions and sketch a coarse two-region path, then a refined local path within each region. Note how the coarse path reduces search effort and how refinement improves movement realism.

Key Takeaway: You can pick a map representation that fits your game, run a simple yet powerful A* search on it, and, when maps grow, add hierarchical pathfinding so NPCs move fast without losing clarity or believability.

Coming up next: Steering, Movement, and Animation Integration

Basic steering behaviors—seek, flee, arrive, and wander—give NPCs direction; combine locomotion with prioritization and blending so movement feels natural; and synchronize physics, root motion, and animation to boost believability. You'll translate the paths we've built here into smooth, believable motion as you explore how movement and perception connect to decisions.

Chapter 5

Steering, Movement, and Animation Integration

By the end of this chapter, you will implement a basic steering system with four behaviors—seek, flee, arrive, and wander—and learn how to blend movement with prioritization and animation so NPCs feel alive, responsive, and believable.

1. Basic steering behaviors: seek, flee, arrive, and wander

Seek: You point the NPC toward a target and steer in that direction. The purpose is to reduce the distance to an objective, such as chasing a player, moving toward a beacon, or closing in on a goal. In practice, you calculate a steering direction toward the target and apply speed based on distance. The closer you get, the less you push the throttle to avoid overshooting.

Flee: You do the opposite. When a threat appears, you push the NPC away from the danger. This is useful for scared characters, retreating allies, or NPCs that must avoid hazards. The key idea is to accelerate away rather than turning crisply at the threat, so the NPC seems to react with natural fear rather than rigid panic.

Arrive: You adjust the NPC's speed so it slows down as it nears the target, preventing a bouncy stop or overshoot. Arrive creates a smooth, believable approach. You determine a stopping distance and scale the speed so the NPC gracefully eases to the target without snapping to a halt.

Wander: You give the NPC a relaxed, exploratory motion when there's no immediate objective. Wander creates the sense of life in an area—the NPC searches the environment, pauses at points of interest, and occasionally changes direction. The aim is to avoid a robotic patrol that never looks around.

Two small examples to illustrate these behaviors

Example A: A guard NPC spots a thief. You apply seek to move toward the thief, drawing closer while adjusting speed so the guard doesn't skid to a stop exactly at the thief's position. As distance shrinks, you dial back speed so the approach feels controlled rather than reckless, producing a believable pursuit.

Example B: A frightened villager hears a loud blast. You trigger flee, turning the villager away from the source of danger and pushing them to a safe distance. If the threat lingers, you blend flee with wander to keep movement natural while the villager scans the area for safety.

How these behaviors relate to one another

You don't rely on a single behavior in isolation. In most scenes, you combine seek, flee, arrive, and wander to create dynamic, responsive movement. A traveler NPC might seek a campsite, arrive smoothly at the camp edge, but wander between tents if there's no pressing target. A predator might seek a player, yet occasionally wander when the player is out of sight, giving the chase a sense of presence rather than a mechanical pursuit.

2. Combining locomotion with prioritization and blending

Prioritization: You decide which motion to apply first in a given moment. If a high-priority condition exists (for example, a threat detected or an obstacle in the path), that behavior should take precedence over lower-priority ones like wandering or idle approaching. Think of prioritization as a hierarchy that protects believable action: safety and goal fulfillment beat casual movement.

Blending: You can blend multiple steering inputs to generate a final direction. Blending is not a simple average; you tune which forces have more influence when. For example, if an NPC must reach a waypoint while avoiding a wall, you blend seek with obstacle avoidance, giving obstacle avoidance a higher weight when close to a barrier and a lower weight when the path is clear.

Local versus global influences: Some behaviors are global (seek toward a moving target anywhere on the map), while others are local (avoid a nearby obstacle). You balance them by changing weights based on distance or situation. A good rule of thumb: raise the weight of safety behaviors when you're near walls or hazards; increase the aggression of goal-seeking when the target is clearly in range and safe to chase.

Two concise micro-cases show how prioritization and blending work in practice

Micro-case 1: A hunter pursuing a fleeing player must chase efficiently but still avoid a cliff edge. Your primary behavior is seek toward the player, but obstacle avoidance has a higher immediate priority when the path is blocked near the cliff. You blend the two so the NPC steers around the obstacle without losing track of the target.

Micro-case 2: A guard patrols a corridor and then a threat is detected behind cover. The guard keeps wandering along the corridor (wander) but temporarily switches to seek when the threat is spotted through a doorway. If the threat becomes a direct danger, flee overrides seek to put distance between the guard and danger.

Practical tips for clean blending

- Start with a simple base: pick one primary behavior (usually seek or wander) and add a secondary behavior with a smaller weight.

- Use a smooth weighting curve. Rather than abrupt changes, ease weights up and down to avoid pops in motion.

- Clip speeds and steer outputs to prevent oscillations. If outputs spike, you'll see jittery movement, which breaks immersion.

- Test with quick silhouettes: do the NPCs act predictably when the target moves unpredictably? If not, adjust the weighting or the timing of transitions.

3. Syncing physics, root motion, and animation for believability

Physics and root motion: When you use physics, the NPC's actual positional updates come from the physics system, not just animation. Root motion uses the movement embedded in the animation itself to drive the character's position and sometimes rotation. The key is to keep physics, animation, and steering in harmony so motion looks consistent, not disjointed.

Animation timing and speed: The rate at which animations play should reflect the steering speed. If the character is moving fast using seek, the run or sprint animation should mirror that pace. If you slow down during arrival, the animation should smoothly transition to a walk or near-idle pose. Constant speed mismatches feel fake; synchronization is the subtle craft that makes movement believable.

Root motion alignment: If you rely on root motion, the actual motion should align with the computed steering direction. When the steering vector points left, the root motion should show a corresponding leftward movement in the animation. If you blend animations, ensure the root motion's translation aligns with the resulting movement to avoid "drift" where the visuals don't match the path.

Collision and contact considerations: Even with smooth steering, your NPC can bump into walls or other units. That's normal in the real world, and your players notice it when it's excessive. Include a light contact response: a tiny bounce or slide along a wall can preserve believability. If the NPC repeatedly collides, revisit the obstacle avoidance weights and the angular speed of turning.

Two micro-cases illustrate syncing physics, root motion, and animation

Micro-case 1: A hunter uses run-root-motion animation while pursuing a player. You ensure the translation from the animation matches the steering direction and the navmesh path. The NPC's feet land in a plausible rhythm while the speed matches the distance to the target, preventing any mismatch between movement and legs.

Micro-case 2: A companion character follows the player with movement that blends into idle waiting in a doorway. The root motion shifts into lighter walking, then stops, while the physics ensures a gentle, believable pause at the threshold.

The blend preserves continuity between motion, frame rate, and the environment's constraints.

Examples and micro-cases in action

Example A: You set up a guard with four steering behaviors: seek toward an intruder, arrive as they close in to a measured distance, wander when no intruder is present, and periodically flee when a loud explosion occurs nearby. The guard's motion shows a purposeful pursuit with natural pauses, then a swift, controlled retreat, all while the animation speeds adjust to match the behavior. The result is a believable patrolling presence that reacts to trouble without looking robotic.

Example B: You pair an ally NPC with a player who often moves diagonally through a narrow hallway. The ally uses seek to keep up but detects a wall nearby. Obstacle avoidance increases, and the speed scales down as the ally nears the corner. The animation shifts from a steady jog to a careful approach, and the root motion aligns so the ally's feet land in sync with the path, producing a convincing, responsive companion.

Exercises

1) Implement the four steering behaviors (seek, flee, arrive, wander) for a simple NPC. Timing: 15 minutes. How to measure progress: the NPC can move toward a target, retreat from a hazard, slow down near the target, and wander when unused.

Watch for overshooting and jitter; successful execution means the NPC transitions smoothly between behaviors as the situation changes.

2) Create a small scene where the NPC must chase a moving target while avoiding a nearby obstacle. Timing: 20 minutes. How to measure progress: track how often the NPC maintains distance without colliding; adjust weights to keep the path readable and stable. If the NPC collides, tweak obstacle avoidance and speed limits.

3) Tie steering to animation by matching the run/walk cycle to the speed of seek and arrive. Timing: 15 minutes. How to measure progress: observe that faster movement uses faster animation; slower movement uses slower

animation. Check for alignment between animation translation and steering direction.

4) Do a quick root motion test in a short corridor. Timing: 10 minutes. How to measure progress: ensure the translated distance from root motion mirrors the steering-driven movement. If drift occurs, adjust the weighting, timing, or drag on the motion to re-align visuals with path.

Troubleshooting quick fixes

- Movement jitters or jittery transitions: reduce abrupt weight changes and apply a small smoothing factor between frames. Ease in and out as you switch behaviors, rather than snapping.

- Overshooting on arrive: shorten the stopping distance and slow the target speed as it gets closer. Ensure a gradual deceleration curve rather than a sudden stop.

- Behavior oscillation: lock a minimum threshold so the NPC doesn't flip between seeking and wandering in tight spaces; use a small hysteresis on weight changes to reduce rapid flipping.

- Obstacle avoidance that causes stalling: ensure there's enough look-ahead distance and a max turn rate that allows the NPC to steer around obstacles without stalling in place.

- Root motion misalignment: verify that the speed of the root motion matches the steering velocity; if not, adjust the animation speed or blend rates so translation matches steering.

- Physics and animation out of sync: keep a consistent update order—steering calculations, then animation, then physics—so outputs reflect in both visuals and movement accordingly.

- Getting stuck near walls: simplify the nav area or add a tiny offset so the NPC doesn't ride the wall edge; ensure obstacle avoidance triggers early enough to prevent contact.

Templates and quick-start tools

- Behavior blending template

Active behaviors: [seek, flee, arrive, wander]

Weights: [seek: 0.6, flee: 0.1, arrive: 0.2, wander: 0.1]

Conditions: [target distance, hazard presence, proximity to walls]

- Movement planning checklist

Objective: move to target with believability

Primary behavior: [seek/arrive]

Secondary behaviors: [obstacle avoidance, wander when idle]

Blend weights: [dynamic, adjust with distance and hazard]

- Quick-start steering plan

Step 1: Define target and hazard positions.

Step 2: Set primary behavior to seek or arrive based on distance.

Step 3: Add obstacle avoidance with a higher weight near barriers.

Step 4: Enable wander when no target is present.

Step 5: Align root-motion animation speeds with steering speed.

Key Takeaway: Use simple steering behaviors thoughtfully, blend them with care, and align animation and physics to create movement that feels intentional and alive rather than scripted.

Coming up next Subtittle: Perception and Situational Awareness

1) Line-of-sight, field-of-view, and auditory sensing systems,

2) Occlusion handling, memory persistence, and target tracking,

3) Filtering sensory input into usable situational data

Chapter 6

Perception and Situational Awareness

You will learn how NPCs perceive their world and turn what they see, hear, and remember into usable information that guides their actions.

Line-of-Sight, Field-of-View, and Auditory Sensing

You start with the basics: line-of-sight is the straight path between an NPC's eyes and a potential thing to notice. If something blocks that path—like a wall, a tree, or a swinging door—the NPC typically cannot see what's on the other side. In games, designers often check this line to decide whether a character can notice another character, an object, or an event. This simple rule creates believable nooks and crannies in your levels.

Field of view is the cone of vision in front of the NPC. Things inside this cone are candidates for noticing you, while things far outside are generally ignored unless something else changes the story. You can imagine field of view as a flashlight beam that sweeps ahead as the character turns its head or body. The important part is not the exact angle but the idea that perception isn't endless. You don't want every action on the map to be instantly visible to every NPC at all times, or players will feel watched and overwhelmed. The balance is to make perception predictable and learnable, so players can plan around it.

Auditory sensing adds another layer. Even if nothing is in the line of sight, a loud sound can catch attention. In games, sounds have a range, and some sounds are more noticeable than others. A stomping foot, a slammed door, or a shout might trigger a reaction even if the source isn't visible. The key idea is that hearing is a separate channel from sight, but the two channels often combine. For example, a guard might hear someone running and then look toward the likely source, using sight to confirm what the ear picked up.

Two short micro-cases help these ideas click. Case A: You hide behind a pillar as a guard walks by. The line-of-sight is broken, so the guard cannot see you, even though you're close. The guard might math the most recent location and keep walking, or pause briefly to check common hiding spots. Case B: You dash across a room in silence. You're inside the field of view, but if you move too fast, you might startle the guard, causing a moment of surprise or a quick turn to check the doorway. In both cases, perception shapes how the guard reacts in real time, and players learn to test those limits to outmaneuver challenges.

A practical note: you do not need fancy tools to implement this. Simple checks work well. When designing, think in terms of three questions for any scene: Is the target within line-of-sight? Is the target inside the field of view cone? Is there a loud or distinctive sound that could reveal the target? If two of these are true, you have a candidate to react to. If all three are true, you've got a strong cue to act quickly. The beauty is that this framework stays predictable while still feeling alive and dynamic.

Occlusion Handling, Memory Persistence, and Target Tracking

Occlusion is anything that hides or blocks view, such as walls, furniture, or even other moving characters. A smart NPC should check not only what is currently visible but also what could be hidden behind obstacles. When line-of-sight is blocked, the NPC doesn't react as if nothing happened; instead, it may enter a search or patrol state to reestablish perception. This behavior makes game worlds feel more like real places, where characters don't instantly forget what they were doing just because something briefly blocked their gaze.

Memory persistence is how long an NPC remembers a prior encounter after the direct cue has disappeared. A quiet memory bakes in a little continuity to the scene. If an NPC has seen you recently, it might still act cautiously, check your last known position, or return to that location later. The exact duration isn't sacred; you simply need a window long enough to create believable follow-up actions without dragging the player through stale consequences.

Target tracking is how an NPC follows a moving target across time. Even when you vanish from view, you may leave a trail that the NPC uses to predict where you might be headed. Think of it as a cautious guess plus an ongoing check: the NPC keeps paying attention to the last known location, adjusts as new information arrives, and periodically re-evaluates the situation. It's a simple, practical trick that prevents NPCs from freezing when the action shifts quickly.

Two micro-cases illustrate these ideas. Case C: You slip around a corner and disappear from direct sight behind a wall, but you were just there a moment ago. The guard may remember your last position and begin a methodical search, walking toward where you were last seen and listening for any footsteps. Case D: You sprint toward a doorway and then pause. The NPC detects the sound and rechecks the doorway, slightly before you step back into sight, creating tension without resorting to a perfect, omniscient detector. In both cases, memory and occlusion help NPCs feel attentive without breaking immersion.

Filtering Sensory Input Into Usable Situational Data

Raw signals—sight lines, sounds, movement—are noisy. The trick is to filter these signals into meaningful, usable data that an NPC can act on. This filtering is the bridge between sensing and decision-making. Start with simple rules: if an object is visible and close, treat it as "seen." If a sound is loud and near, treat it as "heard." If neither, but you previously saw the object, you may still keep a memory flag for a short time.

Combine multiple signals to create clearer outcomes. If something is seen and heard, you gain confidence in the decision to react. If you see something but hear nothing, you might stay cautious but not chase. If you hear something and don't see it, you might investigate the source rather than assuming its exact location. These combinations let you tune how responsive an NPC feels without requiring complex math or heavy processing.

A practical approach is to construct a small perception log or "situational snapshot" for each NPC. Each snapshot records: last seen position, last auditory cue, and a confidence level about what is currently true. Updates happen each frame or on a timed interval, depending on your game's performance needs. The snapshot doesn't demand exhaustive precision; it merely guides the NPC toward sensible actions. The more you practice with these snapshots, the more natural your NPCs become.

Two micro-cases to see this in action. Case E: An archer on a balcony sees a rogue sneaking along the courtyard edge. The archer's snapshot shows recent sighting and a high confidence cue, prompting a cautious aim and ready stance. Case F: A group of guards hears a distant crash. They filter the noise through the perception log, decide it merits investigation, and begin a coordinated sweep toward the sound, even if nothing is clearly visible yet. In both examples, filtering sensory input into a simple, usable state keeps gameplay fluid and understandable for players.

Key Takeaway: Perception is a three-part loop—see, hear, remember—and the mind of your NPCs uses simple filters to turn raw signals into immediate, believable actions.

Coming up next: Decision-Making and Planning Techniques

In the next chapter, you'll explore how NPCs move from sensing the world to deciding what to do. You'll learn Goal-Oriented Action Planning for flexible task sequencing, Utility-based scoring for context-sensitive choices, and how to balance short-term reactions with longer-term plans. This will help you build NPCs that react smartly to changing situations while still feeling consistent and fair to players.

Chapter 7

Decision-Making and Planning Techniques

By the end of this chapter you will be able to design NPC decision-making that flexibly sequences tasks, makes smart choices based on context, and balances fast reactions with longer-term plans.

1. Goal-Oriented Action Planning for flexible task sequencing

You start with a simple idea: the NPC has goals, and it uses a planner to find a path of actions that achieves those goals in the real game world. Think of goals as destinations, like “reach cover,” “secure the objective,” or “help an ally survive.” Actions are the building blocks that move the NPC toward those goals, each with preconditions that must be true before the action can fire and effects that change the world once the action completes. When you put these pieces together, you get a system that can rearrange its steps on the fly as the scene changes.

What this looks like in practice is a small, believable decision process. Your NPC asks: What goal makes sense right now given what I can see, hear, or feel? Which sequence of actions can realistically lead to that goal? The planner then selects a plan—a chain of actions—that will produce the desired outcome, even if the environment shifts in the middle of the plan. This approach gives you a type of adaptability that feels intentional rather than robotic.

A practical takeaway is to separate goals from actions. Goals stay the same long enough to drive consistent behavior; actions are the flexible pieces that connect goals to the world. When you implement this, you'll often see NPCs that adjust their plans when a new threat appears, when their allies need help, or when a resource becomes suddenly scarce.

Example 1: The corner guard and the changing threat

Imagine a guard who wants to keep a corridor clear. The goal is straightforward: “Maintain control of the corridor.” Available actions include “patrol the corridor,” “move to a blind corner,” “call for backup,” and “engage if in range.” If the player steps into view, the planner might choose “pursue the intruder,” but if the intruder is far away or the guard’s health is low, the plan could switch to “fall back to cover” or “signal for reinforcement.” You don’t hard-wire a single path; you build a map of possible routes from any given world state. The system keeps evaluating what goal matters most and what sequence of actions can reliably achieve it, given current conditions.

Example 2: The healer who balances risk and aid

In a squad, a healer's goal might be "keep the team healthy." Actions include "heal ally," "move closer to the frontline," "call for long-range support," or "retreat to safer ground." If a nearby ally needs healing but the healer's own health is dangerously low, the planner can adjust by choosing a safer action—perhaps "retreat to safety" first, then "heal ally from a safer position." The point is not to chase a single line of action but to re-plan as the battle evolves. The goal remains constant, but the action sequence shifts to fit the moment.

Rationale and practical tips

- Start with a small goals map. Pick a few core goals for a given NPC type and map out the action options that could lead to each goal. This keeps the planner manageable and the behavior readable.

- Keep preconditions clean and observable. Use conditions you can reliably detect in-game: line of sight, distance to target, recent damage, proximity to cover, ally status, resources collected, and similar signals.

- Prefer modular actions. Each action should be self-contained and testable. If you can swap in a different action without breaking the whole plan, you've designed a robust system.

- Build in plan invalidation. When a new event dramatically changes the situation (a sudden ambush, a teammate's fall, a door opening), the NPC should reevaluate its goals and replan. This re-planning creates believable responsiveness without needing magic.

Two micro-cases further illustrate how GOAP helps you keep behavior coherent under pressure

Micro-case A: A stealth mission sees a guard's plan pivot on a chance sighting. The guard has the goal "keep the area secure." Actions include "patrol," "check corners," "watch door," and "alert team." If the player is spotted briefly, the guard re-evaluates and moves to "block the doorway" or "call for reinforcements" instead of chasing blindly.

The outcome feels natural because the plan adapts to vision changes, not because a different line of code triggers every time.

Micro-case B: A resource-gathering NPC must decide whether to collect water or guard a camp. The goals are “collect water” or “protect camp.” Actions include “go to water source,” “set camp perimeter,” and “send scout.” If the water source is far away and the camp is under threat, the planner may switch goals or alter the action sequence to “defend first, then collect water later.” This keeps the character useful in multiple situations and avoids dead-end behavior.

2. Utility-based scoring for context-sensitive choices

Utility-based scoring adds a simple, transparent way to choose among several viable actions. Instead of picking actions strictly by pre-planned sequences, the NPC assigns a utility (a kind of usefulness score) to each candidate action in the current moment. The action with the highest utility is chosen. Utilities consider multiple factors: distance to target, danger level, mission priority, resource availability, ally status, and even recent events. The core idea is that each action has a value that reflects how beneficial it would be to perform it right now.

How to set this up in a way that stays readable and tunable

- Define a small set of base utilities for common actions. For example: “attack,” “defend,” “heal,” “retreat,” “gather resource,” “call for help.” Keep the list limited at first so the behavior remains understandable.

- Assign situational multipliers. Then, for each action, multiply the base utility by situational factors: proximity to objective, relative threat, current health, and so on. The result is a single number that can be compared across actions.

- Use a few fixed weights to balance priorities. You’ll often find that a handful of weights (for safety, mission progress, and resource status) can cover a wide range of situations. You can adjust them over time to tune how aggressive, cautious, or cooperative the NPC appears.

- Keep compatibility with GOAP. Utilities don't replace planning; they guide the choice among parallel options that the planner can organize into a plan. The two work together: you plan from goals, and utilities help you pick the most promising action when multiple routes are viable.

A practical way to think about utility

Imagine an NPC who must decide whether to chase an intruder, call for backup, or retreat. Utilities might look like this in plain terms:

- Chase intruder: high if intruder is close and the NPC is strong; low if the NPC is damaged or the intruder is far.

- Call for backup: higher when a group threat is detected or when allies are nearby who can help; lower if everyone is busy elsewhere or if calling would reveal the NPC's position to the intruder.

- Retreat: higher if the NPC is low on health or if backing off increases the chance of the team surviving; lower if staying put keeps an objective within reach.

Two micro-cases demonstrate how utilities shape real in-game behavior

Micro-case 1: The ambush neighbor

A hunter NPC faces an approaching rival. The actions are “ambush from cover,” “signal ally,” and “retreat to safe ground.” The utility calculations weigh proximity to the rival, exposure to danger, and how much time the team has before reinforcements arrive. If the rival is near and the hunter is healthy, “ambush from cover” wins. If the rival closes in and the hunter’s teammates can flank, “signal ally” might take precedence. If reinforcements are arriving and danger is rising, “retreat to safe ground” could be the highest utility to preserve the team for future opportunities. The story you tell with these scores is a world where the hunter adapts, rather than blindly chasing every intruder.

Micro-case 2: The engineer with limited ammo

An engineer NPC must choose between repairing a machine, firing a defensive shot, or moving to a better vantage point. Utilities reflect not just the immediate effect of each action, but how that action contributes to long-term success. If the machine is critical to the mission and ammo is abundant, repair could have a higher utility. If damage is escalating fast and ammo is scarce, retreat or repositioning to maximize cover might win out. These choices feel practical because they're based on concrete, observable factors rather than abstract rules.

Rationale and practical tips

- Start with a handful of actions and a compact scoring rubric. You don't need a million variables to get believable decisions. A few clear, well-chosen factors often do the job.

- Use relative comparisons, not absolute numbers alone. It's often easier to tune by watching outcomes as utilities shift with changing situations.

- Prepare for edge cases. If two actions tie, have a tie-breaker rule such as "prefer actions that preserve health" or "prefer actions that advance the main objective."

- Tie utilities to testable outcomes. If your game often shows odd behavior, check whether high-utility actions prevent progress or cause repetitive patterns. You can adjust the weights or introduce a small randomness to break monotony without breaking realism.

Two micro-cases illustrate how utility scoring brings clarity to action selection

Micro-case A: The turret's dilemma

A turret NPC must decide between shooting, defending, or aiding a nearby ally. Shooting is tempting when the intruder is in range, but if the ally is in danger and the turret can provide protection, defending may yield a higher utility. If the ally's condition improves or the intruder retreats, the turret switches to a different action. The result is a decision pattern that reads as thoughtful rather than mechanical.

Micro-case B: The medic who balances urgency and safety

A medic has to decide between healing a wounded teammate, withdrawing to a safer location to avoid exposure, or gathering supplies. Utilities help weigh urgency (teammate's health), risk (exposure to gunfire), and opportunity (find a better supply cache). The medic's choices feel purposeful—the medic acts to save lives while staying within safe bounds so more teammates can be helped later.

3. Balancing short-term reactions with longer-term plans

You want NPCs to react quickly to immediate changes, but you also want them to act with a sense of purpose that fits the story you're telling. The trick is to create a system where short-term reactions are fast and local, while longer-term plans guide how those reactions accumulate into meaningful behavior over time.

Key ideas to implement

- Define a planning horizon. Decide how far ahead an NPC plans. A short horizon might mean the NPC reacts to what's directly in front of it, while a long horizon encourages strategic moves that align with broader objectives.

- Use plan refresh rates. Some situations demand instant reactions, others benefit from slow, deliberate planning. You can vary how often an NPC recalculates its plan based on the pace of gameplay or the severity of the threat.

- Introduce event-driven interrupts. A sudden event—like an ally falling or a new hazard appearing—should interrupt ongoing plans and trigger a re-planning process. This keeps behavior alive and responsive.

- Keep behavior coherent with a visible through-line. Even when reacting to surprises, the NPC should appear to be pursuing steady goals. If a character sprints around in a panic for no clear reason, players notice and the world feels flimsy.

Two micro-cases show how balancing short-term and long-term thinking shapes NPCs

Micro-case 1: The city guard with a plan

A guard has a weekly patrol route (longer-term plan) but must respond to immediate events like a loud disturbance. The guard's short-term reaction might be to move toward the source of the noise, but the system keeps a long-term plan to complete the patrol if the disturbance turns out to be a false alarm. When the guard helps a distressed citizen, that small action becomes part of a larger narrative about the guard's reputation. The balance creates a believable rhythm: quick responses that don't derail the overarching mission.

Micro-case 2: The scavenger who adapts on the fly

A scavenger NPC is instructed to gather resources while avoiding danger. If a valuable resource appears but enemies are nearby, the scavenger can decide to delay the pickup and instead move to a safer location to wait for the threat to pass. If the danger subsides, the scavenger returns to collect the resource. This pattern—reactive decisions that contribute to longer-term goals—helps the scavenger feel both brave and prudent, like a character with a plan rather than a set of random moves.

Rationale and practical tips

- Keep the balance explicit. Clarify which actions serve short-term reactions and which tie into long-term plans. When players observe both, they'll perceive a coherent character with a believable strategy rather than a string of opportunistic moves.

- Use diagnostic checks. After each scene, review whether the NPC's actions seemed too reactive or too rigid. If the NPC never adapts, increase re-planning frequency or adjust the horizon. If the NPC changes plans too often, extend the planning period or add stronger goal bindings.

- Build in graceful degradation. If a long-term plan becomes impossible (for example, a key objective becomes unreachable), the NPC should fall back to a plausible alternative that still makes sense in the story world.

- Test with varied play styles. Different players push NPCs in different directions. Your balancing should accommodate stealthy players, aggressive players, and players who focus on resource management.

Examples to ground this section in action

Example 1: Short-term reaction with a long-term goal

An archer is tasked with defending a pass (long-term goal). A sudden flurry of melee attackers appears. The archer's short-term reaction is to "fire at the closest danger," quickly reducing the threat.

Meanwhile, the long-term plan remains focused on defending the pass and preserving ammunition for a larger engagement. If the archer's health drops, the long-term plan may shift to "call for help" or "move to higher ground," showing a measured, layered approach to problem-solving.

Example 2: Environmental shift and sustained purpose

In a dungeon, a rogue tries to steal a relic while avoiding guards. The rogue's long-term plan includes "acquire relic" and "exit the dungeon." If a guard unexpectedly spots the rogue, the short-term reaction becomes "evade and hide," but the long-term plan continues to guide decision-making toward the relic. The result is a character who can pivot when attacked but remains driven by a clear objective.

Key Takeaway: When you combine GOAP planning, utility-based scoring, and a thoughtful balance of short-term reactions with longer-term plans, your NPCs feel purposeful, adaptable, and believable rather than repetitive or random.

Coming up next Subtittle: Learning and Adaptation for Games

1) Reinforcement learning basics suited to game constraints,

2) Imitation learning and offline training pipelines,

3) Hybrid approaches: parameter tuning, player modeling, and adaptation

Chapter 8

Learning and Adaptation for Games

You will learn how to use learning and adaptation to make game NPCs smarter while staying within game rules.

1. Reinforcement learning basics suited to game constraints

Reinforcement learning (RL) is a way for an agent to learn by trying actions and watching what happens next. In simple terms, an NPC (the agent) takes an action in the game world, the world (the environment) responds, and the NPC gets feedback called a reward. The agent uses that feedback to decide what to do next time, aiming to get more rewards over time. In games, rewards are usually designed to encourage useful behavior: catching the player, helping a teammate, reaching a goal, or staying alive in a safe way. The overall idea is to shape what the NPC learns so it behaves in ways that feel fair and fun to the player.

When you apply RL to games, you face some practical constraints. First, you need to keep the learning process fast and not too expensive. Games run in real time, so you can't spend hours for one moment of NPC action. A common approach is to train in a separate sandbox or offline, where you let the NPC play many simulated rounds. Then you bring the learned behavior into the real game. Second, you want predictability. Players rely on facing characters that act in ways they can understand and anticipate. So, you set up the training to prefer steady improvement over wild, unpredictable gambits. Third, exploration—the idea of trying new actions to discover better strategies—must be controlled. In a game, too much exploration can ruin the player's experience. You typically limit exploration, or use exploration only in a safe, isolated training phase before you expose the agent to live play.

To make RL work smoothly in a game, you design a simple, well-scoped set of states and actions. The state is what the NPC can "see" at a moment: the player's distance, line of sight, nearby allies, or hazards. The actions are practical choices the NPC can perform: move toward a target, take cover, call for help, or perform a quick attack. The rewards are a compact signal that tells the NPC "this was good" or "this was bad." You want rewards to align with the player's experience: do the NPCs push the player toward fun moments rather than frustrate them with endless stalling or unfair ambushes.

A few plain examples help make this concrete. Example one: a patrol guard learns to intercept a player who slips past certain doors. In training, the guard gets a small reward for getting closer to the player and a bigger reward for successful interception. It earns a tiny negative reward if it loses sight of the player for too long. Over many training rounds, the guard shifts from wandering to patrolling smarter routes and using cover better, and the player notices a more believable chase behavior. Example two: a boss enemy learns attack timing. When the boss uses an effective attack pattern that brings the player into a risk zone, it gets a reward. If the player escapes easily, the reward is smaller. After training, the boss adapts its rhythm to the level's pace so challenges feel fair yet satisfying rather than random.

The practical steps you follow in this section are simple. Start by defining a clear goal for the NPC's behavior. Next, design a reward signal that captures the goal without encouraging bad habits. Then, train in a safe simulator or a paused, controlled game scenario where mistakes don't disrupt players' experiences. Finally, test the learned behavior in the real game, watching for edge cases and making small refinements to rewards or state definitions. This cycle—define, train, test, refine—helps you improve NPC behavior without losing control of the player's experience.

A third point you'll keep in mind is safety and ethics in RL. In games, you're not trying to mirror real life; you're trying to entertain and delight a player. That means avoiding actions that feel cheap, repetitive, or unfair. It also means avoiding policies that could leak into online play in ways players might dislike. The safe path is to keep the learning loop narrow, well-scoped to the game's design, and always with a robust guardrail that prevents extreme or harmful actions from appearing in live play.

Key takeaway from this section: RL can improve how NPCs react and adapt, but you must keep training small, predictable, and aligned with the player's experience to stay fun.

2. Imitation learning and offline training pipelines

Imitation learning uses demonstrations from a human or an already well-tuned script to teach the NPC how to behave. Think of a player or a well-crafted AI scripted by designers. The NPC watches these demonstrations and learns a policy—a map from situations to actions—that imitates the demonstrated behavior. The big win here is safety and speed: you start with solid, human-like behavior without needing to learn everything from scratch in real time.

An offline training pipeline means you collect a bunch of gameplay data, run the learning process on that data, and then bring the trained policy into the game. The advantage is you can use lots of play sessions, with varied styles, to teach the NPC how to respond in many different moments. Since the training happens away from the live game, you avoid dragging down the player's moment-to-moment experience during development.

Two practical examples illustrate how this works. Example one: an archer NPC learns to aim by watching recorded sequences of a player taking shots from different positions. The demonstrations show where to aim, when to release, and how to adjust for distance and wind—if the game has wind. The trained policy reproduces those aiming patterns in new encounters, producing believable archery behavior that feels natural to players. Example two: a guard learns to use cover by studying gameplay clips where players take cover effectively. The NPC adopts similar postures and movement between cover points, creating a sense that the game world is responsive and intelligent without requiring the NPC to discover every strategy by trial and error during live play.

In practice, you keep the pipeline simple. Collect diverse demonstrations, process them into a usable dataset, and train a model that maps game situations to actions. Then validate the policy with a separate set of examples to check generalization. If the policy struggles in new maps or with unseen player tactics, you can augment the dataset with additional demonstrations or perform small post-training adjustments. A common safeguard is to blend imitation with a light amount of on-policy refinement, so the NPC can adjust to the live game while staying anchored in the demonstrated behavior.

A practical note about limitations: imitation learning can reproduce what's in the data, but it may miss ideas the data never showed. If players discover novel strategies, the NPC might not respond as well unless you add a mechanism to learn or adapt beyond the demonstrations. The cure is a hybrid approach, which is the next section's focus.

Key takeaway from this section: Imitation learning gives you a reliable starting point for believable NPC behavior, and offline training lets you harness lots of play data safely before you let NPCs interact dynamically in live games.

3. Hybrid approaches: parameter tuning, player modeling, and adaptation

Hybrid approaches blend the strengths of learning with simple, transparent rules designers can tweak directly. The core idea is to keep the AI flexible enough to feel alive, but predictable enough to be fun and fair. You can adjust how aggressive an NPC is, how quickly it reacts, or how much it seeks cover by tuning parameters. This keeps the behavior legible to players while letting you fine-tune the game feel without re-training from scratch.

Player modeling is the practice of watching how a specific player plays and using that information to tailor NPC behavior. For example, if a player tends to rush in and attack, you can adjust nearby guards to position themselves better for counterattacks. If a player prefers stealth and patience, you can bias NPCs toward more cautious lines of observation. The point is not to spy on players but to create a sense that the game world responds to who is playing.

Adaptation means the game adjusts its difficulty or the NPC's behavior in response to what's happening in a session. A straightforward form is dynamic difficulty: if players perform very well, NPCs might become slightly tougher or more tactical; if players struggle, NPCs ease back a bit to keep the experience enjoyable. The key is to keep changes gradual and visible enough that players feel the experience is responsive, not arbitrary.

Two micro-cases show how hybrids work in practice. Micro-case one: during a siege, the game collects a quick snapshot of player success rates for different enemy tactics. The AI then tweaks a few parameters—like how often enemies switch positions or how long they stay in cover—to keep the siege tense but fair. Micro-case two: in a stealth game, the player's pace and detection missed instances are logged. The next mission uses those logs to adjust a few NPCs' sensitivity to line of sight and noise, so the world feels reactive without being overly punishing.

The practical steps here are small and repeatable. Start with clear, designer-friendly parameters for NPC behavior—things like reaction time, aggression level, and preferred engagement range. Use player modeling data to guide initial defaults, then test with players to see if the feel is right. If the game supports it, set up a controlled feedback loop where the system gently shifts these parameters over time or across levels, keeping the core design intact. Finally, document the logic so future designers can understand why the NPCs behave the way they do, even as you add more learning or hybrid capabilities later.

A practical warning: hybrid approaches work best when you keep the changes conservative and transparent. If you push adaptation too far or make it hard to predict NPC behavior, players may feel the game is cheating or inconsistent. The aim is to support a consistent, enjoyable challenge, not to surprise players with mystery behavior.

Coming up next: You've explored how learning and adaptation can shape individual NPCs and small group dynamics. In the next chapter, you'll dive into Group Behavior, Coordination, and Emergence, including team tactics, shared signals among agents, and how large crowds can create lively, sometimes surprising, patterns in games.

Coming up next

Subtittle: Group Behavior, Coordination, and Emergence

1) Team tactics, role assignment, and inter-agent communication

2) Flocking, crowd simulation, and emergent gameplay patterns

3) Networked synchronization and consistency for multiplayer AI

Key Takeaway: Learning and adaptation empower NPCs to respond to players and environments in smarter ways, but keep a steady balance with predictability and fun.

Coming up next

Subtittle: Group Behavior, Coordination, and Emergence

1) Team tactics, role assignment, and inter-agent communication

2) Flocking, crowd simulation, and emergent gameplay patterns

3) Networked synchronization and consistency for multiplayer AI

Chapter 9

Group Behavior, Coordination, and Emergence

You will learn how groups of NPCs cooperate, how crowds form from simple rules, and how multiplayer AI stays in sync, so your game feels cohesive, believable, and fair across players.

1. Team tactics, role assignment, and inter-agent communication

You build a squad with clear roles, simple rules, and a way for agents to talk without chatter overload. Start by choosing a small roster—leader, scout, defender, and support often work well for many patrols or skirmishes. The leader makes primary calls, the scout looks for threats and reports back, the defender holds chokepoints, and the support provides backup or distraction when needed. The point is not to cram every possible action into one agent; it's to create a predictable pattern your players can learn and exploit or anticipate.

Step 1: Define roles and responsibilities. Decide what each role does in normal, alert, and combat states. Rationale: Well-scoped duties prevent clashes and keep the team moving with a purpose rather than wandering. If an NPC has a clear role, you can reason about the team's behavior more easily when designing encounters.

Step 2: Create decision triggers. Establish simple conditions that trigger role changes, such as "if the leader is out of position, the scout takes lead" or "if a threat appears from behind, the defender shifts to flank protection." Rationale: Small, deterministic triggers keep the team from flipping scripts mid-scene and help you predict outcomes during testing.

Step 3: Build a lightweight communication protocol. Use a few essential signals: a rally call, a target update, a danger alert, and a status broadcast (for example, “hold position,” “advance,” or “seen danger ahead”). Rationale: Too many signals slow things down and waste CPU; concise, essential messages maintain clarity and performance.

Step 4: Tie behavior to roles with rule-based behavior trees or simple FSMs. Each role should have its own flow of actions that respond to the same high-level situation in a predictable way. Rationale: Separate, role-specific rules minimize conflict and help you reason about the team’s flow when you watch a replay or test a scenario.

Step 5: Test with small skirmishes and steady-state patrols. Start with four agents in a corridor and two in a doorway. Rationale: Small tests reveal whether roles clash, messages collide, or agents ignore orders, and they let you fix issues before you scale up.

Two micro-cases to see these ideas in action:

- Case A: A four-NPC patrol guards a doorway. The leader calls "Hold," the defender wedges the doorway, the scout peeks for threats beyond the entrance, and the support keeps an eye on the corridor for flankers. If a loud noise happens, the scout immediately reports back, the leader orders a quick regroup, and the defender shifts to block new openings. You can observe how the team preserves a doorway as a unit and still stays responsive to surprises.

- Case B: A small rescue team in a city ruin. The leader directs a two-step approach: scout first, then enter with a shielded line. The defender remains central to push against cover while the support provides distraction fire. The team communicates only essential updates, so the chaos remains manageable and readable.

Troubleshooting notes for this section:

- Problem: Two NPCs give conflicting orders. Quick fix: designate a single “order authority” signal and ensure others heed it; keep a short list of order types to avoid duplication.

- Problem: Messages flood the network or the CPU. Quick fix: limit broadcasts to changes in state or position updates rather than constant pings; every message should have a purpose.

- Problem: Roles do not adapt to new players or new map layouts. Quick fix: build a small "environment awareness" cue that feeds back into role decisions, so the team adapts without rewiring every rule.

Examples and micro-cases show how these ideas look in real gameplay: a guard squad, a search-and-rescue team, and a siege defense. In each, look for clear role behavior, minimal, purposeful communication, and smooth transitions when conditions change.

Exercises:

1) Create a four-NPC patrol with roles and one leader for a narrow corridor. Time: 20 minutes. Measure progress by observing that all four agents perform their roles and respond to a sudden threat within two seconds of detection.

2) Run a mock "breach and clear" with a five-agent team. Time: 25 minutes. Measure progress by watching for no more than two conflicting orders at once and a visible, predictable role shift when the leader is "taken out."

3) Add a new role to the squad (e.g., a medic or a hacker) and test how the team reassigns duties. Time: 30 minutes. Measure progress by confirming

the new role never dominates the team's behavior and the original roles still function smoothly.

4) Create a one-minute replay where you adjust communication to reduce chatter. Time: 15 minutes. Measure progress by counting the number of messages that actually change the plan and ensuring none are wasted.

Key Takeaway: Clear roles and a lean, shared language let teams of NPCs work like a real squad, even when things get noisy or unexpected.

Transition: Now that you see how teams coordinate, let's watch how larger groups behave when movement becomes a collective phenomenon.

Coming up next, Subtittle: Flocking, crowd simulation, and emergent gameplay patterns.

2. Flocking, crowd simulation, and emergent gameplay patterns

You uncover how simple rules at the individual level can create believable crowd motion and surprising group behaviors. The idea is to give each NPC a few local rules and trust that the group will produce a coherent whole, without scripting every moment of the crowd.

Step 1: Implement basic flocking rules: cohesion (move toward the average position of neighbors), separation (avoid crowding), and alignment (move in the same direction as neighbors). Rationale: These three rules yield smooth, natural movement without heavy path planning.

Step 2: Add obstacle avoidance and boundary handling. NPCs should steer around walls, barriers, and open edges instead of colliding or piling up or wandering off-map edges. Rationale: Real crowds don't walk through walls, and believable navigation requires awareness of the environment.

Step 3: Introduce goal bias and personal preferences. Give individuals a soft preference to move toward goals (e.g., exit doors or gathering points) and a personal space preference that can vary a little between agents. Rationale: Small differences help avoid robotic uniformity and produce more varied, lifelike motion.

Step 4: Tune sensing radius and update frequency. Keep neighborhood checks local to maintain performance; the update rate should balance smoothness with CPU load. Rationale: Too-wide sensing or too-frequent updates slow the game and may cause jitter; the art is efficiency with believable behavior.

Step 5: Observe emergent patterns and shape the space. Use corridors, bottlenecks, and obstacles to create natural lines, waves, and pauses. Rationale: Emergence happens when local rules interact with the terrain; you can guide patterns through level design and rule tuning, not by scripting every move.

Two micro-cases show the power of simple rules:

- Case A: A market square fills with shoppers moving in loosely connected streams. People slow near corners, form queues at stalls, and automatically avoid collisions, producing a lively but readable crowd flow without a central director.

- Case B: A group of villagers fleeing a danger, funneling through a narrow street and forming a living, shifting line that moves toward the safe zone. The line shifts as obstacles appear, and the crowd adapts without explicit instructions.

Troubleshooting notes:

- Problem: Crowds bunch up at narrow passages. Quick fix: increase separation slightly or introduce a slightly stronger goal bias toward the open space after the passage.

- Problem: Behavior feels repetitive or robotic. Quick fix: add small random perturbations to headings or slight variation in personal space to break symmetry.

- Problem: Pathfinding eats resources for large crowds. Quick fix: simulate crowds in local neighborhoods with shared momentum classes and reduce global pathfinding calls; rely on local steering for most agents.

Examples and micro-cases provide a sense of scale: a village square, a crowded bridge, and a market street. You'll notice how the crowd's motion becomes a character of its own, shaped by the terrain and the local rules, rather than by a single director.

Exercises:

1) Build a 20-agent crowd in an open plaza with two exits. Time: 20 minutes. Measure progress by observing that agents reach an exit with minimal overlaps and natural spreading.

2) Add a sudden obstacle (a fallen cart) and watch the wave of rearrangement. Time: 15 minutes. Measure progress by how quickly the crowd re-routes and how many agents settle into new lines without chaos.

3) Create a narrow corridor with people moving in one direction and a counterflow on a side path. Time: 25 minutes. Measure progress by the formation of a natural lane and a visible balance between orderly flow and emergent variation.

4) Introduce a few agents with slightly different personal space settings. Time: 15 minutes. Measure

progress by reduced robotic feel and more organic crowd motion.

Key Takeaway: Small, local rules plus thoughtful terrain design can create believable crowds and emergent, engaging patterns without handcrafting every move.

Transition: With groups behaving responsibly and crowds feeling alive, you're ready to tackle multiplayer consistency and synchronization. Coming up next, Subtittle: Networked synchronization and consistency for multiplayer AI.

3. Networked synchronization and consistency for multiplayer AI

You ensure that what players see is fair and the same for everyone, even when voices and connections differ. The goal is to keep AI decisions deterministic where it matters and to handle non-determinism gracefully so everyone shares the same experience.

Step 1: Use an authoritative server model. The server makes the final decisions about critical actions, states, and outcomes to prevent cheating and to keep the game fair for all players. Rationale:

Authority reduces disagreement across clients and ensures consistency.

Step 2: Replicate essential AI state to all clients. Send compact state updates for positions, goals, and current actions at a steady tick rate. Rationale: Regular updates keep clients synchronized without flooding the network.

Step 3: Implement client-side prediction and smooth interpolation. Clients should render plausible movement between server updates while still receiving authoritative corrections. Rationale: Prediction makes the game feel responsive even under network latency.

Step 4: Manage randomness with fixed seeds and deterministic subsystems. If an NPC uses random choices, seed the randomness so all clients can reproduce the same sequence when needed. Rationale: Consistent randomness prevents divergence across clients, which is essential for fairness.

Step 5: Test across network conditions and keep debugging tools handy. Simulate latency, jitter, and dropped packets to see how AI behavior holds up and to identify desynchronization risks. Rationale: Real-world testing reveals edge cases that synthetic tests miss and helps you tune timing budgets.

Examples:

- Case A: In a co-op mission, AI patrols on all clients follow the server's authoritative path but interpolate their motion so players see smooth movement regardless of small delays.

- Case B: In a competitive match, enemy squads appear to react to player actions consistently on every device because the server handles target selection and posture while clients render the results with prediction.

Troubleshooting notes:

- Problem: Clients drift out of sync after a large lag spike. Quick fix: apply a one-time reconciliation pass when the next authoritative update arrives and use interpolation to re-sync positions.

- Problem: Random events cause inconsistent outcomes. Quick fix: base randomness on a shared seed or deterministic pseudo-random generator controlled by the server.

- Problem: Too many state updates saturate the network. Quick fix: compress updates, send only delta changes, and throttle updates during calm periods.

Tools and templates you can use:

- A simple state update template: keep position, velocity, current action, and a short status flag per NPC; only send if any value changed.

- A basic client prediction template: apply server-provided velocity to render, then correct with server data when available.

- A lag budget checklist: target tick rate, maximum packet size, and acceptable latency window; track these in testing sessions.

- A deterministic seed management template: store seeds on the server and reuse them on clients to keep behavior in sync.

Exercises:

1) Set up a three-NPC squad in a networked scene. Time: 40 minutes. Measure progress by confirming that all clients share identical action queues after a server update, within a small interpolation window.

2) Introduce 150 ms simulated latency and observe AI continuity. Time: 30 minutes. Measure progress by smooth movement and minimal position jumps after reconciliation.

3) Implement a simple randomized decision that uses a server seed. Time: 25 minutes. Measure progress by verifying identical outcomes across clients for the same seed and scenario.

4) Create a logging panel that records discrepancies between server and client states during a playthrough. Time: 20 minutes. Measure

progress by reducing desync events to near-zero after adjustments.

Key Takeaway: A strong, authoritative core with careful replication and smoothing keeps multiplayer AI fair, predictable, and responsive across players and networks.

Coming up next, Transition: In the Tools, Testing, Optimization, and Deployment chapter, you'll learn how to instrument AI, visualize behavior, run automated tests, profile performance, and wire these practices into your game pipeline. Subtittle: Tools, Testing, Optimization, and Deployment

1) Instrumentation, visualization, and automated tests for AI

2) Profiling, optimization strategies, and deterministic simulations

3) Data-driven content, scripting workflows, and engine integration

Chapter 10

Tools, Testing, Optimization, and Deployment

By the end of this chapter, you will be able to instrument AI behavior, visualize what your agents are doing, run automated tests, profile for performance, and wire up data-driven content, scripting workflows, and engine integration so your game AI runs smoothly and predictably.

1. Instrumentation, Visualization, and Automated Tests for AI

Instrumentation means putting tiny data collectors into your AI code so you can see what happens under the hood. You don't need every micro-detail, but you do need enough to answer questions like: Which decision did the NPC make? How long did that decision take? How often does the agent switch states? The goal is to gather consistent, lightweight data that won't drag the game down.

Start with a simple set of metrics. Track events such as "perception check," "decision made," "state transition," and "path recalculation." Record a timestamp with each event and a lightweight counter for how many times it happens in a given stretch of play. Keep data local when possible and batch it for later analysis to avoid bogging down the frame rate.

Visualization makes the data meaningful. In-game overlays work well for quick feedback: draw paths with colored lines to show where an NPC intends to move, colorize alerts (green for calm, yellow for suspicious, red for danger), and show small glyphs near agents to indicate which behavior is active. External dashboards—simple, readable charts that show decisions per minute, average decision time, and the frequency of perception checks—help you spot trends across many tests and different levels. The point is not to replace careful observation but to augment it with clear, interpretable visuals.

Automated tests give you a safety net. Build tests that verify core AI behaviors in repeatable ways. Start with unit tests for individual components (for example, "does the perception module flag a valid target within range?"). Add integration tests that simulate a sequence (such as "patrol → detect → chase → lose target → return to patrol") and confirm the overall flow remains correct. Use fixed seeds for randomness in tests to keep outcomes predictable, so a test failure points to an actual issue, not a random fluctuation.

Include smoke tests that run a quick loop of AI updates in a controlled scene to ensure nothing crashes during normal play.

Two micro-cases to illustrate:

- Micro-case A: A guard NPC with two states—patrol and chase. Instrument the transitions and count how many times the NPC moves from patrol to chase per minute. If the rate is erratic or too frequent, you know something is causing jitter (perhaps a perception check firing too often). Visualize the patrol path and the chase trigger lines to confirm the condition that flips the state is behaving as expected.

- Micro-case B: An enemy that detects the player with line-of-sight. Draw debug rays for the sight checks and log when detections occur. If detections fire when the player is hidden, you've got a perception bug to fix. The combination of visuals and logs helps you identify exactly where the misfire happens.

Templates and tools you can adapt now:

- Instrumentation Template: Metric name, source (which module), event type, timestamp, value, and a short description. Use concise, consistent names so you can aggregate data later.

- Visualization Plan: What to show on-screen (paths, states, alerts) and what to export (metrics dashboards). Decide refresh rate so overlays are informative but not distracting.

- Automated Test Plan: Test name, objective, scenario, expected result, and a pass/fail criterion. Include both isolated unit tests and small, repeatable integration tests.

Common pitfalls and quick fixes:

- Instrumentation slows the game. Fix: sample only a subset of events, or bucket data and write in chunks during pauses or loading screens.

- Too many metrics, hard to read. Fix: start with a focused core set (decisions per minute, average decision time, state transitions) and add more later only if needed.

- Tests fail sporadically. Fix: force deterministic seeds in tests and isolate timing dependencies.

Exercises (2–4 short, timed, progress-measuring tasks you can do now)

- Exercise 1: Implement a small instrumentation pocket for a single NPC. Add three metrics (decision time, state transitions, and perception checks). Run a 5-minute test scene and record the averages. Compare two different NPCs and note any outliers.

- Exercise 2: Create an on-screen visualization for a single AI agent. Draw its current path as a line, its active state as a color badge, and a tiny marker when it detects something. Do a 10-minute playthrough and judge how clearly you can interpret its behavior from the overlay alone.

- Exercise 3: Write a basic automated test that simulates a perception event and checks that the correct state transition happens. Use a fixed seed for any randomness. Run the test three times and ensure the result is consistent.

- Exercise 4: Build a tiny dashboard snippet (even a local, simple chart will do) that shows decisions per minute and average decision time for the test scene. Re-run after a small change and note whether the numbers move in the expected direction.

Tools and templates you can copy or adapt:

- AI Instrumentation Checklist: List of metrics, data sources, sampling rate, and where to store logs.

- Visualization Overlay Template: On-screen elements to render (path lines, state badges, detection lines) and how to color code them.

- Auto-Test Skeleton: A plain structure with test name, scenario, inputs, expected outputs, and a success criterion.

2. Profiling, Optimization, and Deterministic Simulations

Profiling is about finding where time and memory are spent in your AI, so you can focus your optimization where it matters. Profiling helps you see the real bottlenecks, not just the ones you guess at. Start by measuring the AI update time per agent and the total time spent in perception, decision-making, and pathfinding within a frame. Note how your numbers change when you add more NPCs, more complex navigation, or more data-driven decisions.

Optimization ideas you can apply in practical steps:

- Reduce update frequency. If AI can tolerate a small delay, decouple its update rate from the frame rate. Run AI logic every few frames instead of every frame, then interpolate for on-screen visuals. This often yields big gains with little perceptible change in feel.

- Cut unnecessary recomputations. Cache results where it's safe, reuse previous path results when the target hasn't moved much, and avoid repeating expensive checks in tight loops.

- Use spatial partitioning and data structures to prune work. Group agents into zones or grids so each AI only considers nearby players or other agents. This reduces the number of perception checks and decisions that must be made each frame.

- Minimize allocations in hot paths. Dynamic memory allocation inside update loops can trigger slow garbage collection. Prefer pre-allocated buffers, object pooling, and simple stack allocations where possible.

- Leverage determinism for predictability. If you need consistent behavior across runs (important for testing and multiplayer consistency), fix seeds for randomness and use deterministic updates on circuits where possible.

Deterministic simulations matter when you want reproducible results. A deterministic AI behaves the same way given the same start conditions and inputs. This makes testing reliable and helps with debugging across machines and sessions.

Two micro-cases to illustrate:

- Micro-case C: A crowd of 30 NPCs with steering and collision avoidance. Profiling reveals a hot spot in the navmesh query loop. You resolve this by batching navmesh queries, caching nearby path results, and updating paths only when a neighbor changes position beyond a threshold. The result is smoother movement and fewer stuttery decisions without losing the sense of crowd behavior.

- Micro-case D: A tactical game AI that makes complex plans using a mix of randomization and rule-based choices. You enforce determinism by seeding the random generator at the start of each planning episode and by using fixed time steps for all AI decisions. Re-running the same scenario produces the same plan, which makes debugging and balancing much easier.

Practical strategies for profiling and optimization:

- Profiling plan: Run a repeatable scene, capture frame-by-frame timing for perception, decision, and movement. Note spikes and determine if they come from a single NPC, a module, or a particular map area.

- Optimization plan: Prioritize reducing bottlenecks first (the biggest time sinks). If pathfinding is heavy, consider caching, hierarchical pathfinding, or making fewer path queries per frame. If perception is costly, cap the number of checks per agent or stagger checks over several frames.

- Deterministic simulation plan: Use a fixed time step for all AI updates. Remove or control random variation in critical loops. Log a trace of decisions to verify consistency across runs.

Exercises (2–4 short, timed, progress-measuring tasks you can do now)

- Exercise 5: Profile a small scene with multiple NPCs. Note the top three time sinks and estimate the impact of each on frame time. Try one quick optimization (e.g., reduce update frequency or cache a result) and re-profile to compare.

- Exercise 6: Implement a deterministic planning cycle for a simple AI. Set a fixed seed and use a consistent time step. Run the same scenario three times and verify the decisions match.

- Exercise 7: Test how a crowd scales. Increase the number of NPCs in a scene and watch CPU usage, memory, and decision density. Identify a point where performance starts to degrade noticeably and brainstorm a simple fix.

Tools and templates you can copy or adapt:

- Profiling Plan Template: Target frame rate, metrics to collect, tools to use, and a schedule for testing.

- Optimization Checklist: Common techniques (update rate, caching, spatial pruning, memory management) with quick win examples.

- Deterministic Simulation Guide: Steps to fix seeds, time steps, and reproducibility checks.

3. Data-Driven Content, Scripting Workflows, and Engine Integration

Data-driven content means letting data files shape AI behavior instead of hard-coding every rule. This makes balancing, tuning, and testing much faster. You can adjust aggressiveness, detection radii, flee distances, and preferred routes by changing values in data files, not in code. When you separate data from logic, you empower designers to experiment and iterate quickly.

Scripting workflows are about arranging AI behavior using scripts or a lightweight scripting language. Scripts let you assemble behaviors, test new sequences, and prototype ideas without touching core engine code. Scripting also helps with rapid iteration, enabling designers and programmers to collaborate smoothly. Keep scripts clean and modular so they're easy to reuse and test.

Engine integration is about how AI fits into your game engine's systems. Tie your AI to core processes—event handling, physics, animation, and rendering—through well-defined interfaces. Use an event bus or blackboard pattern to share information between systems without creating tight couplings. Keep a clear boundary between AI logic and engine timing to maintain stability and portability across platforms.

Two micro-cases to illuminate these ideas:

- Micro-case E: A friendly NPC uses data-driven parameters for its stance toward the player. In a level data file, you adjust a single parameter labeled "trust_threshold" that changes how often the ally assists or blocks the player's path. The same AI code responds differently as you tune the parameter, and you can experiment with balance in hours rather than days.

- Micro-case F: A patrol route generated by a script. The script reads a list of waypoints, adds some randomness for variation, and then assigns the route to a group of NPCs. Designers can modify the script or the waypoint list to craft different experiences while the programmers leave the core navigation intact.

Templates and checklists you can use now:

- Data-Driven Content Template: Parameter name, description, valid range, default value, and which AI modules read it. Include an example level file snippet showing how a value affects behavior.

- Scripting Workflow Checklist: What to script, the order of execution, error handling, and tests to run after changes.

- Engine Integration Checklist: Interfaces to implement, data to expose, how to subscribe to events, and a quick-start example scene.

Common pitfalls and quick fixes:

- Data drift: Your data files diverge from what the code expects. Fix by locking the data schema, adding validation, and versioning the data alongside the code.

- Script brittleness: Scripts become hard to maintain as AI grows. Fix by modularizing scripts, writing small, testable units, and documenting expected inputs and outputs.

- Engine coupling: AI logic becomes tangled with engine specifics. Fix by defining clean interfaces and keeping AI logic agnostic of rendering or physics details.

- Tooling friction: Designers and programmers clash over workflows. Fix by creating lightweight, well-documented templates and encouraging small, incremental changes rather than big rewrites.

Exercises (2–4 short, timed, progress-measuring tasks you can do now)

- Exercise 8: Create a simple data-driven parameter. Add a value called "aggressiveness" to a data file and wire it to an NPC's decision timer. Change the value step by step and observe how the behavior shifts in a controlled test scene. Record observations.

- Exercise 9: Write a tiny script that generates patrol routes from a list of waypoints with a random variation. Run the script in three test scenes and compare route lengths and variability.

- Exercise 10: Implement a basic engine integration for an AI module. Use a simple event system to pass a perception event to a decision component and a follow-up action to the movement system. Validate that events flow correctly across systems in a test scene.

Tools and templates you can copy or adapt:

- Data-Driven Content Template: Data item, description, valid range, default, a mapping to AI behavior, and a sample impact on behavior.

- Scripting Workflow Template: Step-by-step flow for authoring, testing, and deploying a script; error handling and rollback plan.

- Engine Integration Template: Core interfaces, event names, expected data shapes, and a minimal example scene to verify end-to-end flow.

Troubleshooting quick guide (across all three parts)

- AI runs but feels inconsistent. Check instrumentation, confirm fixed seeds, and verify data drift isn't changing decisions mid-scene.

- Performance dips after a new feature. Re-profile to confirm the new feature is the bottleneck, then roll back or optimize with caching and update-rate adjustments.

- Data-driven changes break behavior in some levels but not others. Validate data with a level-wide test and ensure fallbacks are present when data is missing.

Key Takeaway: You can make AI faster, more reliable, and easier to tune by instrumenting behavior, profiling performance, and separating data and scripts from core code.

Transition: With the tools to observe and improve AI in hand, you're ready to explore the architectures and data models that organize these systems. In the next chapter, you'll learn how to structure AI with modular data, agents, and communication patterns so your tools can scale cleanly across games.

Dear Reader,

Thank you for exploring this series focused on failures and the power of comeback stories. If you find value in these stories and believe in the importance of embracing setbacks as part of growth, we appreciate your support. Please consider sharing a positive review on the platform where you accessed this series.

Your feedback helps spread the message, inspiring more young readers to see challenges as opportunities and to believe in their potential. We understand that mistakes happen, and we thank you for your understanding.

www.ingramcontent.com/pod-product-compliance
Lightning Source LLC
LaVergne TN
LVHW022204200926
848481LV00006B/1845

* 9 7 9 8 2 9 5 5 3 5 4 3 7 *